SRI SRI PARAMAHANSA YOGANANDA
Gurudeva and Founder
Yogada Satsanga Society of India/
Self-Realization Fellowship

The
SCIENCE
of
RELIGION

by
SRI SRI PARAMAHANSA YOGANANDA

With a Preface by
DOUGLAS AINSLIE, B.A., M.R.A.S.

Yogoda Satsanga Society of India
FOUNDED 1917
Paramahansa Yogananda

This Indian Edition, 1990
Seventh Impression, 2017

 An authorized publication of Yogoda Satsanga Society of India/Self-Realization Fellowship
The Yogoda Satsanga Society of India name and emblem shown above appear on all YSS books, recordings, and other publications, assuring the reader that a work originates with the society established by Sri Sri Paramahansa Yogananda and faithfully conveys his teachings.

The trade dress of this book is a trademark of Self-Realization Fellowship

Published in India by
YOGODA SATSANGA SOCIETY OF INDIA
Yogoda Satsanga Math
21, U. N. Mukherjee Road
Dakshineswar, Kolkata 700 076

Printed in India by
Kailash Paper Conversion Pvt. Ltd.
Ranchi 834001

ISBN 978-81-89535-16-2

Distributed by:

 Jaico Publishing House   Manjul Publishing House

Also available from Yogoda Satsanga Society of India, Paramahansa Yogananda Path, Ranchi 843001, Jharkhand and at Yogada Satasanga Ashrams and dhyana kendras throughout India.

For his piety, generosity to many worthwhile movements, and pioneer patronage in the establishment of a Yogoda Satsanga residential school for boys in Ranchi, Jharkhand, this book is lovingly inscribed to the late honorable Maharaja Sri Manindra Chandra Nundy of Kasimbazar, West Bengal.

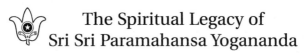

The Spiritual Legacy of Sri Sri Paramahansa Yogananda

His Complete Writings, Lectures, and Informal Talks

Paramahansa Yogananda founded Yogoda Satsanga Society of India (YSS) in 1917 and Self-Realization Fellowship (SRF) in 1920 to disseminate his teachings worldwide and to preserve their purity and integrity for generations to come. A prolific writer and lecturer from his earliest years in America, he created a renowned and voluminous body of works on the yoga science of meditation, the art of balanced living, and the underlying unity of all great religions. Today this unique and far-reaching spiritual legacy lives on, inspiring millions of truth seekers all over the world.

In accord with the express wishes of the great Guru, Yogoda Satsanga Society of India / Self-Realization Fellowship has continued the ongoing task of publishing and keeping permanently in print *The Complete Works of Paramahansa Yogananda.* These include not only the final editions of all the books he published during his lifetime, but also many new titles — works that had remained unpublished at the time of his passing in 1952, or which had been serialized over the years in incomplete form in Yogoda Satsanga Society of India / Self-Realization Fellowship's magazine, as well as hundreds of profoundly inspiring lectures and informal talks recorded but not printed before his passing.

Paramahansa Yogananda personally chose and trained those close disciples who have headed the Yogoda Satsanga Society of India / Self-Realization Fellowship Publications Council since his passing, and gave them specific guidelines for the preparation and publishing of his teachings. The members of the YSS / SRF Publications Council (monks and nuns who have taken lifelong vows of renunciation and selfless service) honour these guidelines as a sacred trust, in order that the universal message of this beloved world teacher will live on in its original power and authenticity.

The Yogoda Satsanga Society of India / Self-Realization Fellowship emblem (shown above) was designated by Paramahansa Yogananda to identify the nonprofit society he founded as the authorized source of his teachings. The YSS / SRF name and emblem appear on all YSS / SRF publications and recordings, assuring the reader that a work originates with the organization founded by Paramahansa Yogananda and conveys his teachings as he himself intended they be given.

— YOGODA SATSANGA SOCIETY OF INDIA/SELF-REALIZATION FELLOWSHIP

Contents

Preface

By Douglas Grant Duff Ainslie
(1865-1952)
*(English statesman, poet, and philosopher; delegate to
International Congress of Philosophy,
Harvard University)*

This small book offers the clue to the universe.

Its value is beyond estimation in words, since between these narrow covers is to be found the flower of the *Vedas* and *Upanishads*, the essence of Patanjali, foremost exponent of the Yoga philosophy and method, and the thought of Shankara, greatest mind that ever dwelt in mortal body, placed for the first time within reach of the multitude.

This is the deliberate statement of one who has at last found in the East, after many wanderings, the solution to the riddles of the world. The Hindus have revealed to the whole world the Truth. And this is only natural, when we consider that more than five thousand years ago, while the forefathers of Briton and Gaul, Greek and Latin, were roaming the vast forests of Europe in search of food, true barbarians, the Hindu was already engaged in pondering the mystery of life and death, which now we know to be one.

The essential point to be remarked about Paramahansa Yoganandaji's teaching, in contradistinction to that of European philosophers, such as Bergson, Hegel, and others, is that it is not speculative, but practical, even when dealing with the utmost reaches of metaphysics. The reason is that the Hindus, alone of mankind, have penetrated behind the veil, and possess the knowledge, which is really not philosophical, i.e., wisdom-loving, but wisdom itself. For, when expressed in terms of verbal dialectic, this knowledge must perforce lay itself open to the criticism of philosophers whose life it is, as Plato said, to be constantly engaged in discussion. The truth cannot be expressed in words, and when words are used, even by a Shankara, acute minds can always find a loophole for attack. The finite, in fact, cannot contain the infinite. Truth is not an eternal discussion; it is Truth. It follows that only by actual personal realization, by practice of method such as Paramahansa Yoganandaji offers, can Truth ever be known beyond doubt.

All the world desires bliss, as Paramahansaji says and proves, but most are deluded by desire for pleasure. Buddha himself never stated more clearly that it is desire, ignorantly followed, which leads to the morass of misery in which the vast majority of mankind is help-lessly floundering.

But Buddha failed to state with equal clearness the fourth of the four modes of attaining to the state of bliss that we all desire. This fourth mode is by far the easiest, but needs for its practical achievement the guidance of an expert. This expert is now among us to give to the West the technique, the simple rules, which have been handed down for centuries from the ancient philosophers of India, and which lead to realization or the state of permanent bliss.

This direct contact is always stressed as of great importance in Hindu thought and practice. Until our day, it has been out of reach of all but those fortunate enough to dwell in India. Now that we have it in the West, actually at our door, he would indeed be unwise who should avoid or neglect to make trial of a practice which of itself is intensely blissful — "far more purely blissful than the greatest enjoyment that any of our five senses or the mind can ever afford us," as Paramahansa Yoganandaji truthfully declares, and adds, "I do not wish to give anyone any other proof of its truth than is afforded by his own experience."

The first step can be taken by reading this small book; the others needful for reaching the complete state of bliss will follow naturally.

I conclude by quoting a few lines from my "John of Damascus," in which I attempt poetically to suggest what in this book is attained. The Buddha speaks, who for us is Paramahansa Yoganandaji, since "Buddha" means simply, "He who knows."

Long have I wandered, long, he sang,
Bound by the chains through lives and pains
Innumerable, and felt the fangs
Of self on fire, of fierce desire.

Found, it is found, the Cause, he sang,
Of self on fire, of wild desire.
No house, O Architect, for me
Again can ever builded be.

Shattered are thy rafters, scattered
Are thy roof timbers utterly:
No house thou buildest more for me.
Mine is Nirvana, mine; it lies
Within my reach, before mine eyes.
Now, if I will it, now, I may
Pass now eternally away
To bliss eternal, leave no trace
Of me in this or other place.

But love I bear thee, love; and stay,
Humanity, for the sole sake,
With mine own hands the bridge to make,
Which, if thou cross, thou too shall'st gain
Freedom from birth and death and pain,
And thus eternal bliss attain.

We have the bridgemaker among us. With his own hands he will build the bridge, if we truly wish him so to do.

London, England
February, 1927

Foreword

Decades before the current interest in Eastern psychology and religion, Sri Sri Paramahansa Yogananda (1893-1952) began his life's work of bringing India's timeless spiritual science to the Western world. In 1920 he was invited to the United States as India's representative to an international conference of world religious leaders in Boston. The lecture he delivered on that occasion, his maiden speech in America, was published soon after as *The Science of Religion.* Since then it has been published in seven additional languages, and is used as a reference work in colleges and universities.

The Science of Religion is a profoundly simple and concise exposition of the common goal of all true religions, and the four main paths that lead to its attainment. It is a universal message, based not on dogmatic beliefs, but on direct insight into Reality, gained through the practice of ancient scientific techniques of meditation.

THE SCIENCE OF RELIGION

Introduction

The purpose of this book is to outline what should be understood by religion, in order to know it as universally and pragmatically necessary. It also seeks to present that aspect of the idea of the Godhead which has a direct bearing on the motives and actions of every minute of our lives.

It is true that God is infinite in His nature and aspects; and it is also true that to prepare a chart detailing, so far as is consistent with reason, what God is like, is only an evidence of the limitations of the human mind in its attempt to fathom God. Still, it is equally true that the human mind, in spite of all its drawbacks, cannot rest perfectly satisfied with what is finite. It has a natural urge to interpret what is human and finite in the light of what is superhuman and infinite — what it feels but cannot express, what within it lies implicit but under circumstances refuses to be explicit.

Our ordinary conception of God is that He is superhuman, infinite, omnipresent, omniscient, and the like. In this general conception there are many variations. Some call God personal, some see Him as impersonal. The point emphasized in this book is that whatever conception we have of God, if it does not influence our daily conduct, if everyday life does not find an inspiration from it, and if it is not found universally necessary, then that conception is useless.

If God is not conceived in such a way that we cannot do without Him in the satisfaction of a want, in our dealings with people, in earning money, in reading a book, in passing an examination, in the doing of the most trifling or the highest duties, then it is plain that we have not felt any connection between God and life.

God may be infinite, omnipresent, omniscient, personal, and merciful, but these conceptions are not sufficiently compelling to make us try to know Him. We may as well do without Him. He may be infinite, omnipresent, and so forth, but we have no immediate and practical use for those conceptions in our busy, rushing lives.

We fall back on those conceptions only when we seek to justify, in philosophical and poetical writings, in art or in idealistic talks, the finite craving for something beyond; when we, with all our vaunted knowledge, are at a loss to explain some of the most common phenomena of the universe; or when we get stranded in the vicissitudes of the world. "We pray to the Ever-Merciful when we get stuck," as the Eastern maxim has it. Otherwise, we seem to get along all right in our workaday world without Him.

These stereotyped conceptions appear to be the safety valves of our pent-up human thought. They explain Him, but do not make us seek Him. They lack motive power. We are not necessarily *seeking* God when we call Him infinite, omnipresent, all-merciful and omniscient. These conceptions satisfy the intellect, but do not soothe the soul. If respected and cherished in our hearts, they may broaden us to a certain extent — may make us moral and resigned toward Him. But they do not make God our own — they are not intimate enough. They place Him aloof from everyday concerns of the world.

These conceptions savor of outlandishness when we are on the street, in a factory, behind a counter, or in an office. Not because we are really dead to God and religion, but because we lack a proper conception of them — a conception that can be interwoven with the fabric of daily life. What we conceive of God should be of daily, nay hourly, guidance to us. The very conception of God should stir us to seek Him in the midst of our daily lives. This is what we mean by a pragmatic and compelling conception of God. We should take religion and God out of the sphere of belief into that of daily life.

If we do not emphasize the necessity of God in every aspect of our lives and the need of religion in every minute of our existence, then God and religion drop out of our intimate daily consideration and become only a one-day-in-a-week affair. In the first part of this work an attempt is made to show that in order to understand the real necessity of God and religion we must throw emphasis on that conception of both which is most relevant to the chief aim of our daily and hourly actions.

This book also aims to point out the universality and

unity of religion. There have been different religions in different ages. There have been heated controversy, long warfare, and much bloodshed over them. One religion has stood against another, one sect has fought with another. Not only is there a variety in religions, but there is also a wide diversity of sects and opinions within the same religion. But the question arises, When there is one God, why should there be so many religions?

It may be argued that particular stages of intellectual growth and special types of mentality belonging to certain nations, owing to different geographical locations and other extraneous circumstances, determine the origin of different religions, such as Hinduism, Mohammedanism, and Buddhism for the Asiatics, Christianity for the Westerners, and so forth. If by religion we understand only practices, particular tenets, dogmas, customs, and conventions, then there may be grounds for the existence of so many religions. But if religion means *primarily* God-consciousness, or the realization of God both within and without, and *secondarily* a body of beliefs, tenets, and dogmas, then, strictly speaking, there is but one religion in the world, for there is but one God.

The different customs, forms of worship, tenets, and conventions may be held to form the grounds for the origins of different denominations and sects included under that one religion. If religion is understood in this way, then and then only may its universality be maintained; for we cannot possibly universalize particular customs and conventions. Only the element common to

SRI SRI MAHAVATAR BABAJI
Guru of Sri Sri Lahiri Mahasaya

SRI SRI LAHIRI MAHASAYA
(Shyama Charan Lahiri)
Sri Yukteswar Giri
Guru of Sri Sri Swami

SRI SRI SWAMI
SRI YUKTESWAR GIRI
Guru of Sri Sri
Paramahansa Yogananda

SUCCESSORS TO PARAMAHANSA YOGANANDA

(Left to Right) Sri Sri Rajarsi Janakananda, spiritual head and president of Yogoda Satsanga Society of India/Self-Realization Fellowship 1952–1955. Sri Sri Daya Mata succeeded Rajarsi Janakananda in February 1955, serving for more than 55 years until her passing in 2010. Sri Sri Mrinalini Mata, another close disciple of the great master chosen and trained by him as one of those to lead his work after his passing, is the current president and spiritual head of YSS/SRF.

all religions may be universalized; we may ask everyone to follow and obey it. Then may it be truly said that religion is not only necessary but universal as well. Everyone may follow the same religion, for there is but one — the universal element in all religions being one and the same.

I have tried to show in this book that *as God is one, necessary to all of us, so religion is one, necessary and universal.* Only the roads to it may differ in some respects at the beginning. As a matter of fact, it is illogical to say that there are two religions, when there is but one God. There may be two denominations or sects, but there is only one religion. What we now call different religions should be known as different denominations or sects under that one universal religion. And what we now know as different denominations or sects should be specified as different branch cults or creeds. If we once know the meaning of the word "religion," which I am going to discuss presently, we shall naturally be very circumspect in the use of it. It is only the limited human point of view that overlooks the underlying universal element in the so-called different religions of the world, and this overlooking has been the cause of many evils.

This book gives a psychological definition of religion, not an objective definition based on dogmas or tenets. In other words, it seeks to make religion a question of our whole inward being and attitude, and not a mere observance of certain rules and precepts.

PART 1

The Universality, Necessity, and Oneness of Religion

The Common Goal of Life

First we must know what religion is; then only may we judge whether it is necessary for all of us to be religious.

Without necessity there is no action. Every action of ours has an end of its own for which we perform it. People of the world act variously to accomplish various ends; there is a multiplicity of ends determining the actions of men in the world.

But is there any common and universal end of all the actions of all the people of the world? Is there any common, highest necessity for all of us, which prompts us to all actions? A little analysis of the motives and ends of men's actions in the world shows that, though there are a thousand and one proximate or immediate ends of men in regard to the particular calling or profession that they take up, the ultimate end — which all other ends merely subserve — is the avoidance of pain and want, and the attainment of permanent Bliss. Whether we can permanently avoid pain and want, and obtain Bliss, is a separate question; but as a matter of fact, in all our actions we obviously try to avoid pain and to gain pleasure.

Why does a man serve as an apprentice? Because he wishes to become an expert in a certain business. Why does he engage in that particular business? Because money can be earned therein. Why should money be earned at all? Because it will satisfy personal and family wants. Why should wants be fulfilled? Because pain will thereby be removed and happiness be gained.

As a matter of fact, happiness and Bliss are not the same thing. We all aim at Bliss, but through a great blunder we imagine pleasure and happiness to be Bliss. How that has come to be so will be shown presently. The ultimate motive is really Bliss, which we feel inwardly; but happiness — or pleasure — has taken its place, through our misunderstanding, and pleasure has come to be regarded as the ultimate motive.

Thus we see that the fulfillment of some want; removal of some pain, physical or mental, from the slightest to the acutest; and the attainment of Bliss form our ultimate end. We may not question further why Bliss is to be gained, for no answer can be given. That is our ultimate end, no matter what we do — enter a business, earn money, seek friends, write books, acquire knowledge, rule kingdoms, donate millions, explore countries, look for fame, help the needy, become philanthropists, or embrace martyrdom. And it will be shown that the seeking of God becomes a real fact to us when our true end is kept rigorously in view. Millions may be the steps, myriads may be the intermediate acts and motives; but the ultimate motive is always the same — to attain permanent Bliss, even though it be through a long chain of actions.

Man usually likes to go along the chain to get to the final end. He may commit suicide to end some pain, or perpetrate murder to get rid of some form of want or pain or some cruel heart-thrust, thinking he will thereby attain a real satisfaction or relief, which he mistakes for Bliss. But the point to notice is that here, too, is the same working (though wrongly) toward the ultimate end.

Someone may say, "I do not care anything about pleasure or happiness. I live life to accomplish something, to achieve success." Another says: "I want to do good in the world. I do not care whether I am in pain or not." But if you look into the minds of these people, you will find that there is the same working toward the goal of happiness. Does the first man want a success that has in its achievement no pleasure or happiness? Does the second want to do good to others, yet himself get no happiness in doing it? Obviously not. They may not mind a thousand and one physical pains or mental sufferings inflicted by others, or arising out of situations incidental to the pursuit of success or the doing of good to others; but because the one finds great satisfaction in success, and the other intensely enjoys the happiness of doing good to others, the former seeks success, and the latter seeks others' good, in spite of incidental troubles.

Even the most altruistic motive and the sincerest intention of advancing the good of humanity, for its own sake, have sprung from the basic urge for a chastened personal happiness, approaching Bliss. But it is not the happiness of a narrow self-seeker. It is the happiness of a broad seeker of that "pure self" that is in you and me and all. This happiness is Bliss, a little alloyed. So with pure Bliss as a personal motive for altruistic action, the altruist is not laying himself open to the charge of narrow selfishness, for one cannot himself have pure Bliss unless he is broad enough to wish and seek it for others, too. That is the universal law.

A Universal Definition of Religion

So, if the motives for the actions of all men are traced farther and farther back, the ultimate motive will be found to be the same with all — the removal of pain and the attainment of Bliss. This end being universal, it must be looked upon as the most necessary one. And what is universal and most necessary for man is, of course, religion to him. Hence, *religion necessarily consists in the permanent removal of pain and the realization of Bliss, or God.* And the actions that we must adopt for the permanent avoidance of pain and the realization of Bliss or God are called religious. If we understand religion in this way, then its universality becomes obvious. For no one can deny that he wants to avoid pain permanently and attain permanent Bliss. This must be universally admitted, since none can gainsay its truth. Man's very existence is bound up with it.

All want to live because they love religion. Even if a man committed suicide it would be because he loved religion, too; for by doing that he thinks he will attain a happier state than he finds while living. At any rate, he thinks he will be rid of some pain that is bothering him. In this case his religion is crude, but it is religion, just the same. His goal is perfectly right, the same that all persons have; for all of them want to obtain happiness, or Bliss. But his means is unwise. Because of his ignorance, he does not know what will bring him to Bliss, the goal of all men.

What It Means To Be Religious

Thus, in one sense every man in the world is religious, inasmuch as everyone is trying to get rid of want and pain, and to gain Bliss. Everyone is working for the same goal. But in a strict sense only a few in the world are religious, for only a few in the world, though they have the same goal as all others, know the most effective means for removing, permanently, all pain or want — physical, mental, or spiritual — and gaining true Bliss.

The true devotee cannot hold a rigidly narrow

orthodox conception of religion, though that conception is, in a remote way, connected with the conception I am bringing out. If for some time you do not go to church or temple, or attend any of its ceremonies or forms, even though acting religiously in your daily life by being calm, poised, concentrated, charitable, squeezing happiness from the most trying situations, then ordinary people of a pronounced orthodox or narrow bent will nod their heads and declare that, although you are trying to be good, still, from the point of view of religion, or in the eyes of God, you are "falling off," as you did not of late enter the precincts of the holy places.

While of course there cannot be any valid excuse for permanently keeping away from such holy places, there cannot, on the other hand, be any legitimate reason for one's being considered more religious for attending church, if at the same time one neglects to apply in daily life the principles that religion upholds, that is, those that make ultimately for the attainment of permanent Bliss. Religion is not dovetailed with the pews of the church, nor is it bound up with the ceremonies performed therein. If you have an attitude of reverence, if you live your daily life always with a view to bringing undisturbed Bliss-consciousness into it, you will be just as religious out of the church as in it.

Of course this should not be understood as an argument for forsaking the church, which is usually a real help in many ways. The point is that you should put forth just as much effort outside the church hours to gain eternal happiness as you forego while from the pews you are passively enjoying a sermon. Not that listening is not a good thing, in its way; for it certainly is.

Religion "Binds" Us to Benevolent Laws

The word "religion" is derived from the Latin *religare*, to bind. What binds, whom does it bind, and why? Leaving aside any orthodox explanation, it stands to reason that it is "we" who are bound. What binds us? Not chains or shackles, of course. Religion may be said to bind us by rules, laws, or injunctions only. And why? To make us slaves? To disallow us the birthright of free thinking or free action? That is unreasonable. Just as religion must have a sufficient motive, so its motive in "binding" us must also be good. What is that motive? The only rational answer we can give is that religion binds us by rules, laws, injunctions in order that we may not degenerate, that we may not be in misery — bodily, mentally, or spiritually.

Bodily and mental suffering we know. But what is spiritual suffering? To be in ignorance of the Spirit. It is present always, though often unnoticed, in every limited creature, while bodily and mental pain come and go. What other motive of the word "binding" than the above may we ascribe to religion that is not either nonsensical or repelling? Obviously other motives, if any, must be subservient to the one given.

Is not the definition of religion already given consistent with the above-mentioned motive of the word "binding," the root meaning of religion? We said that religion, in part, consists in the permanent avoidance of pain, misery, suffering. Now, religion cannot lie merely in getting rid of something, such as pain; it must also lie in getting hold of something else. It cannot be purely negative, but must be positive, too. How can we permanently get away from pain without holding to its opposite — Bliss? Though Bliss is not an exact antonym of pain, it is, at any rate, a positive consciousness to which we can cling in order to get away from pain. We cannot, of course, forever hang in the air of a neutral feeling that is neither pain nor the reverse. I repeat that religion consists not only in the avoidance of pain and suffering, but also in the attainment of Bliss, or God (that Bliss and God are synonymous, in one sense, will be explained later).

By looking, then, into the motive of the root meaning of religion (binding) we arrive at the same definition of religion we reached by the analysis of man's motive for action.

Religion Is a Question of Fundamentals

Religion is a question of fundamentals. If our fundamental motive is the seeking of Bliss, or happiness, if there be not a single act we do, not a single moment we live, that is not determined ultimately by that final motive, should we not call this craving the most deep-seated one in human nature? And what can religion be if it is not somehow intertwined with the deepest-rooted craving of human nature? Religion, if it is to be anything that has life value, must base itself on a life instinct or craving. This is an *a priori* plea for the conception of religion set forth in this book.

If one replies there are many other human instincts (social, self-preservative, and so forth) besides a craving for happiness, and asks why we should not interpret religion in the light of those instincts, too, the answer is that those instincts are either subservient to the instinct of seeking happiness or are too indissolubly connected with the latter to affect substantially our interpretation of religion.

To revert once more to the former argument, *that which is universal and most necessary to man is religion to him.* If what is most necessary and universal is not religion to him, what then can it be? That which is most accidental and variable cannot be it, of course. If we try to make money the one and only thing requiring attention in life, then money becomes religion to us — "the dollar is our God." The predominant life motive, whatever it may be, is religion to us.

Leave aside here the orthodox interpretation, for principles of action — not intellectual profession of dogmas or observance of ceremonies — determine without need of our personal advertisement what religion we have. We need not wait for either the theologian or the minister to name our sect or religion for us — our principles and actions have a million tongues to tell it to us and to others.

The significant part of it is that back of whatsoever thing we worship with blind exclusiveness is always one fundamental motive. That is, if we make money, business, or obtaining the necessities or luxuries of life the be-all and end-all of our existence, still, back of our actions lies a deeper motive: we seek these things in order to banish pain and bring happiness. This fundamental motive is humanity's real religion; other secondary motives form pseudo-religions. Because religion is not conceived in a universal way, it is relegated to the region of clouds, or is considered by many people to be a fashionable diversion for women, or for the aged and feeble.

Universal Religion Is Pragmatically Necessary

Thus we see that Universal Religion (or religion conceived in this universal way) is practically or *pragmatically* necessary. Its necessity is not artificial or forced. Though in the heart its necessity is perceived, yet unfortunately we are not always fully alive to it. Had we been so, pain would long since have disappeared from the world. For ordinarily what a man thinks to be really necessary he will seek at all hazards. If the earning of money is thought by a man to be really necessary for the support of his family, he will not shrink from running into dangers to secure it. It is a pity we do not consider religion to be necessary in the same way. Instead, we regard it as an ornament, a decoration, and not a component part of man's life.

It is also a great pity that although the aim of every man in this world is necessarily religious, inasmuch as he is working always to remove want and attain happiness, yet owing to certain grave errors he has been misdirected and led to consider the true religion, the definition of which we have just given, as of minor importance.

What is the cause of this? Why do we not perceive the real necessity in place of the apparent unimportance? The answer is: the wrong ways of society and our own sense attachments.

It is the company we keep that determines for us the necessity we feel for different things. Consider the influence of persons and circumstances. If you wish to orientalize an Occidental, place him in the midst of the Asiatics; or if you want to occidentalize an Oriental, plant him among Europeans — and mark the results. It is obvious, inevitable. The man of the West learns to like the customs, habits, dress, modes of living and thought, and manner of viewing things of the East, and the man of the

East comes to like those of the West. The very standard of truth seems to them to vary.

Upon one thing, however, most people will agree, and that is that their worldly life, with its cares and pleasures, weal and woe, is worth living. But of the necessity for the Universal Religion few or none will ever remind us, and so we are not quite alive to it.

It is a truism that man seldom looks beyond the circle in which he is placed. Whatever falls within his own circle he justifies, follows, imitates, emulates, and feels to be the standard of thought and conduct. What is beyond his own sphere he overlooks or lessens the importance of. A lawyer, for instance, will praise and be most attentive to what concerns law; other things will, as a rule, have less importance to him.

The pragmatical or practical necessity of the Universal Religion is often understood as merely a theoretical necessity, religion being considered an object of intellectual concern. If we know the religious ideal merely through our intellect, we think we have reached this ideal and that we are not required to live it or realize it.

It is a great mistake on our part to confuse pragmatical necessity with theoretical necessity. Many would perhaps admit, on a little reflection, that Universal Religion is surely the permanent avoidance of pain and the conscious realization of Bliss, but few understand the importance and practical necessity that this religion carries with it.

PART 2

Pain, Pleasure, and Bliss: Their Differences

The Ultimate Cause of Pain and Suffering

Now it is necessary for us to investigate the ultimate cause of pain and suffering, mental and physical, in the avoidance of which the Universal Religion partly consists.

First of all we should assert, from our common universal experience, that we are always conscious of ourselves as the active power performing all of our mental and bodily acts. Indeed we are performing many different functions — perceiving, thinking, remembering, feeling, acting, and so forth. Yet underlying these functions we can perceive that there is an "ego" or "self," which governs them and thinks of itself as substantially the same through all its past and present existence.

The Bible says, "Know ye not that ye are the temple of God, and that the Spirit of God dwelleth in you?"* All of us as individuals are so many reflected spiritual Selves of

* I Corinthians 3:16.

18

the universal blissful Spirit — God. Just as there appear many images of the one sun, when reflected in a number of vessels full of water, so is mankind apparently divided into many souls, occupying these bodily and mental vehicles, and thus outwardly separated from the one universal Spirit. In reality, God and man are one, and the separation is only apparent.

Now, being blessed and reflected spiritual Selves, why is it that we are utterly unmindful of our blissful state and are instead subject to physical and mental pain and suffering? The answer is that the spiritual Self has brought on itself this present state (by whatever process it may be) by identifying itself with a transitory bodily vehicle and a restless mind. The spiritual Self, being thus identified, feels itself sorry for or delighted at a corresponding unhealthy and unpleasant or healthy and pleasant state of the body and mind. Because of this identification, the spiritual Self is being continually disturbed by their transitory states.

To take even the figurative sense of identification: a mother who is in deep identification with her only child suffers and feels intense pain merely by the very hearing of her child's rumored or real death, whereas she may feel no such pain if she hears of the death of a neighboring mother's child with whom she has not identified herself. Now we can imagine the consciousness when the identification is real and not figurative. Thus *the sense of identification with the transitory body and rest-less mind is the source or root-cause of our spiritual Self's misery.*

Understanding that identification of the spiritual Self with the body and mind is the primary cause of pain, we should now turn to a psychological analysis of the immediate or proximate causes of pain and to the distinction between pain, pleasure, and Bliss.

The Immediate Causes of Pain

Because of this identification, the spiritual Self seems to have certain tendencies — mental and physical. Desire for the fulfillment of these tendencies creates want, and want produces pain. Now these tendencies or inclinations are either natural or created, natural tendencies producing natural wants and created tendencies producing created wants.

A created want becomes a natural want in time, through habit. Of whatever sort the want may be, it gives pain. The more wants we have, the greater the possibilities of pain; for the more wants we have, the more difficult is it to fulfill them, and the more that wants remain unfulfilled, the greater is the pain. Increase desires and wants, and pain is also increased. Thus if desire finds no prospect of immediate fulfillment, or finds an obstruction, pain immediately arises.

And what is desire? It is nothing but a new condition of

"excitation" which the mind puts on itself—a whim of the mind created through company. Thus *desire, or the increase of conditions of excitation of the mind, is the source of pain or misery,* and also of the mistake of seeking to fulfill wants by first creating and increasing them, and then by trying to satisfy them with objects instead of lessening them from the beginning.

It might appear that pain is sometimes produced without the presence of previous desire—for example, pain from a wound. But we should observe here that the desire to remain in a state of health, which consciously or subconsciously is present in our mind and is crystallized into our physiological organism, is contradicted in the above case by the presence of the unhealthy state, namely, the presence of the wound. Thus when a certain exciting condition of the mind in the form of a desire is not satisfied or removed, pain results.

As desire leads to pain, so it leads also to pleasure, the only difference being that in the first case, want involved in desire is not satisfied; while in the second case, want involved in desire seems to be satisfied by the presence of external objects.

But this pleasurable experience, resulting from the fulfillment of the want by objects, does not remain but dies away, and we retain only the memory of the objects that seemed to have removed the want. Hence, in future, desire for those objects brought in by memory revives, and there arises a feeling of want, which, if unfulfilled, again leads to pain.

Pleasure Is a Double Consciousness

Pleasure is a double consciousness — made up of an "excitation consciousness" of possession of the thing desired, and of the consciousness that pain for want of the thing is felt no more. There is an element of both feeling and thought in it. This latter "contrast consciousness," that is, the entire consciousness (how I felt pain when I did not have the desired object, and how I now have no pain, as I have obtained the thing I wanted), is what mainly constitutes the charm of pleasure.

Hence we see that consciousness of want precedes — and consciousness of the want's being fulfilled enters into — pleasurable consciousness. Thus it is want and the fulfillment of want with which the pleasure consciousness is concerned. It is mind that creates want and fulfills it.

It is a great mistake to regard a certain object as pleasurable in itself and to store the idea of it in the mind in the hope of fulfilling a want by its actual presence in the future. If objects were pleasurable in themselves, then the same dress or food would always please everyone, which is not the case.

What is called *pleasure* is a creation of the mind — *it is a deluding excitation consciousness, depending upon the satisfaction of the preceding state of desire and upon present contrast consciousness.* The more a thing is thought to excite pleasurable consciousness, and the more the desire for it is harbored in the mind, the greater the possibility of hankering after the thing itself, the presence of which is thought to bring a pleasurable consciousness and its absence a sense of want. Both of these states of consciousness lead ultimately to pain.

So, if we are really to lessen pain, we are, as far as possible, to free the mind gradually from all desire and sense of want. If desire for a particular thing, supposed to remove the want, is banished, deluding excitation consciousness of pleasure does not arise, even if the thing is somehow present before us.

But instead of lessening or decreasing the sense of want, we habitually increase it and create new and various wants in the satisfying of one, resulting in a desire to fulfill them all. For instance, to avoid the want of money we start a business. In order to carry on the business we have to pay attention to thousands of wants and necessities that the carrying on of a business entails. Each want and necessity in turn involves other wants and more attention, and so on.

Thus we see that the original pain involved in want of money is a thousand times multiplied by the creation of other wants and interests. Of course it is not meant that the running of a business or earning of money is bad or unnecessary. The point is that the desire to create greater and greater wants is bad.

Mistaking the Means for the End

If, in undertaking to earn money for some end we make money our end, our madness begins. For the means becomes the end and the real end is lost sight of. And so again our misery commences. In this world everyone has his duties to perform. Let us, for the sake of convenience, review the former instance.

The family man has to earn money to support his family. He starts a certain business and begins to attend to the details that will make it successful. Now, what often happens after a time? The business goes on successfully and money perhaps accumulates until there is much more than is necessary for the fulfillment of his wants and those of his family.

Now one of two things happens. Either money comes to be earned for its own sake and a peculiar pleasure comes to be felt in hoarding, or it may happen that the hobby of running this business for its own sake persists or increases the more. We see that in either case the means of quelling original wants — which was the end — has become an end in itself: money or business has become the end.

Or it may happen that new and unnecessary wants are created and an effort is made to meet them with "things."

In any case our sole attention drifts away from Bliss (which we, by nature, mistake for pleasure and the latter becomes our end). Then the purpose for which we apparently started a business becomes secondary to the creation or increase of conditions or means. And at the root of creation or increase of conditions or means there is a desire for them which is an excitation or feeling, and also a mental picture of the past when these conditions gave rise to pleasure.

Naturally the desire seeks fulfillment by the presence of these conditions: when it is fulfilled, pleasure arises; when not fulfilled, pain arises. And because pleasure, as we remarked already, is born of desire and is connected with transitory things, it leads to excitation and pain when there is a disappearance of those things. That is how our misery commences.

To put it briefly: from the original purpose of the business, which was the removal of physical wants, we turn to the means — either to the business itself or to the hoarding of wealth coming out of it — or sometimes to the creation of new wants; and because we find pleasure in these we are swept away into pain, which, as we pointed out, is always an indirect outcome of pleasure.

What is true of the earning of money is also true of every action of the world. Whenever we forget our true end — the attainment of Bliss or the state, condition, or mode of living eventually leading to it — and direct our sole attention to the things which are mistakenly thought to be the means or conditions of Bliss, and turn them into ends — then our wants, desires, and excitations go on increasing, and we are started on the road to misery or pain.

We should never forget our goal. We should put a hedge round our wants. We should not go on increasing them more and more, for that will bring misery in the end. I do not mean, however, that we should not satisfy necessary wants, arising out of our relation to the whole world, or become idle dreamers and idealists, ignoring our own essential part in promoting human progress.

To sum up: pain results from desire, and in an indirect way also from pleasure, which stands as a will-o'-the-wisp to lure people away into the mire of wants to make them ever miserable.

Thus we see that desire is the root of all misery, which arises out of the sense of identification of the Self with mind and body. So what we should do is to *kill attachment by doing away with the sense of identification*. We should break the cord of attachment and identification only. As appointed by the Great Stage Manager, we should play our parts on the stage of the world with the whole mind, intellect, and body, but remain inwardly as unaffected or unruffled by pleasure and pain consciousness as are the players on an ordinary stage.

Bliss-Consciousness Arises With
Severing of Body Identification

When there is dispassion and severing of identification, Bliss-consciousness arises in us. As long as you are human you cannot but have desires. Being human, how then can you realize your divinity? First have rational desires, then stimulate your desire for nobler things, all the while trying to attain Bliss-consciousness. You will feel that the cord of your individual attachment to various desires is being automatically snapped.

That is to say, from the calm center of Bliss you will ultimately learn to *disown* your own petty desires and to feel only those which seem to be urged in you by a great law. Thus Jesus Christ said, "Not my will, but Thine, be done."*

When I say that to attain Bliss is the universal end of religion, I do not mean by Bliss what is usually called pleasure, or that intellectual satisfaction which arises from the fulfillment of desire and want and which is mixed with an excitation, as when we say we are pleasurably excited. In Bliss there is no excitement, nor is it a contrast consciousness: "My pain or want has been removed by the presence of such and such objects." It is a consciousness of perfect tranquillity — a consciousness of our calm nature unpolluted by the intruding consciousness that pain is no more.

---

* Luke 22:42.

An illustration will make the point clear. I have a wound, and feel pain; when healed, I feel pleasure. This pleasurable consciousness consists of an excitation or feeling, and a constant thought-consciousness that I am no longer feeling the pain of the wound.

Now, the man who has attained Bliss, even though he might receive a physical wound, will feel, when healed, that his state of tranquillity had neither been disturbed when the wound existed, nor regained when it was healed. He feels that he is passing through a pain-pleasure universe with which he really has no connection, and which can neither disturb nor heighten the tranquil or blissful state, which flows on within him without ceasing. This state of Bliss is free from both inclinations and excitement involved in pleasure and pain.

There is a positive and a negative aspect in Bliss-consciousness. The negative aspect is the absence of pleasure-pain consciousness; the positive one is the transcendental state of a superior calm, including within itself the consciousness of a great expansion and of "all in One and One in all." It has its degrees. An earnest truth-seeker gets a little taste of it; a seer or a prophet is filled with it.

Pleasure and pain having their origin in desire and want, it should be our duty — if we wish to attain Bliss — to banish all desire except the desire for Bliss, our real nature. If all our improvements — scientific, social, and political — are guided by this one common universal end (removal of pain) why should we bring in a foreign something (pleasure) and forget to be durably fixed in what is tranquillity or Bliss?

Inevitably, he who enjoys the pleasure of health will sometimes feel the pain due to ill health, because pleasure depends upon a condition of the mind, namely, the idea of health. To have good health is not bad, nor is it wrong to seek it. But to have attachment to it, to be inwardly affected by it, is what is objected to. For to be so means entertaining desire, which will lead to misery.

We must seek health not for the pleasure in it but because it makes the performance of duties and the attainment of our goal possible. It will, some time or other, be contradicted by the opposing condition, ill health. But Bliss depends upon no particular condition, external or internal. *It is a native state of the Spirit.* Therefore it has no fear of being contradicted by any other condition. It will flow on continually forever, in defeat or success, in health or disease, in opulence or poverty.

PART 3

God as Bliss

The Common Motive for All Actions

The foregoing psychological discussion about pain, pleasure, and Bliss, with the help of the following two examples, will make clear my conception of the highest common necessity and of the Godhead, which was touched upon incidentally at the beginning.

I remarked at the outset that if we made a close observation of the actions of men, we should see that the one fundamental and universal motive for which man acts is the avoidance of pain and the consequent attainment of Bliss, or God. The first part of the motive, the avoidance of pain, is something we cannot deny, if we observe the motives of all the good and bad actions performed in the world.

Take the case of a person who wishes to commit suicide, and that of a truly religious man who has dispassion for the things of the world. There can be no doubt about the fact that both of these men are trying to get rid of the pain which is troubling them; both are trying to put an end to pain permanently. Whether they are successful or not is a different question, but so far as their motives are concerned there is unity.

But are all actions in this world *directly* prompted by the desire for the attainment of permanent Bliss, or God, the second part of the common motive for all actions? Does the evildoer have for his immediate motive the attainment of Bliss? Hardly. The reason for this was pointed out in the discussion about pleasure and Bliss. We found that because of the identification of the spiritual Self with the body, it has fallen into the habit of indulging in desires and the consequent creation of wants. These desires and wants lead to pain, if not fulfilled — and to pleasure, if fulfilled — by objects.

But here occurs a fatal error on the part of man. When a want is fulfilled, man gets a pleasurable excitement and, through a sad mistake, fixes his eye solely upon the objects that create this excitement, and supposes them to be the main causes of his pleasure. He entirely forgets that he had formerly an excitation in the form of desire or want in his own mind, and that later he had another excitation in his mind superseding the first one, in the form of pleasure, which the coming of objects seems to produce. So, as a matter of fact, one excitation arose in the mind and was superseded by another in the same mind.

Outward objects are only the occasions — they are not causes. A poor person's desire for delicacies may be satisfied by an ordinary sweetmeat, and this fulfillment will give rise to pleasure. But the desire for delicacies on the part of a rich person may perhaps be satisfied only by the best of pastries, and the fulfillment will also give the same amount of pleasure. Then does pleasure depend on outward objects, or on the state of mind? Surely the latter.

But pleasure, as we said, is an excitation. Therefore it is never justifiable to drive away the excitation in desire by another excitation, namely, that felt in pleasure. Because we do this, our excitations never end, and so our pain and misery never cease.

Only Bliss-Consciousness Can Effectively Put Excitation to Rest

What we should do is to *set at rest* the excitation that is in desire and not fan or continue it by excitation in pleasure. This setting at rest is rendered possible in an effective way only by Bliss-consciousness, which is not callousness but a superior stage of indifference to both pain and pleasure. Every human being is seeking to attain Bliss by fulfilling desire, but he mistakenly stops at pleasure; so his desires never end, and he is swept away into the whirlpool of pain.

Pleasure is a dangerous will-o'-the-wisp, and yet it is this pleasurable association that becomes our motive for future actions. This has proved to be as deceptive as a mirage in the desert. Since pleasure, as was said before, consists of excitation-consciousness plus contrast-consciousness that the pain is now no more, when we aim at it instead of at Bliss, we prepare ourselves for running headlong into that cycle of ignorant existence which brings pleasure and pain in never-ending succession. We fall into terrible distress because of the change in our angle of vision from Bliss to pleasure.

Thus we see that though the true aim of mankind is the avoidance of pain and the attainment of Bliss, man, owing to a fatal error, while trying to avoid pain pursues a deluding something named pleasure, mistaking it for Bliss.

That the attainment of Bliss and not pleasure is the universal and highest necessity is indirectly proved by the fact that man is never satisfied with one object of pleasure. He always flies from one to another: from money to dress, from dress to property, thence to conjugal pleasure — there is a restless continuity. And so he is constantly falling into pain, even though he wishes to avoid it by the adoption of what he deems proper means. Yet an unknown and unsatisfied craving seems ever to remain in his heart.

But a religious man (the second example that I proposed to show) always wishes to adopt proper religious means by which he can come in contact with Bliss, or God.

Of course when I say that God is Bliss, I mean also that

He is ever-existent and that He is also *conscious* of His blissful existence. And when we wish Eternal Bliss or God, it is implied that with Bliss we also wish eternal, immortal, unchangeable, ever-conscious existence. That all of us, from the highest to the lowest, desire to be in Bliss has been proved *a priori,* and by a consideration of the motives and acts of men.

To repeat the argument in a slightly different way: suppose some higher being should come to us and say to all people of the earth, "You creatures of the world! I will give you eternal sorrows and misery along with eternal existence; will you take that?" Would anyone like the prospect? Not one. All want eternal Bliss *(Ananda)* along with eternal existence *(Sat).* As a matter of fact, consideration of the motives of the world also shows there is no one but would like to have Bliss.

Similarly, no one likes the prospect of annihilation; if it is suggested, we shudder at the idea. All desire to exist permanently *(Sat).* But if we were given eternal existence without the *consciousness* of that existence, we would reject that. For who is there that would embrace existence in sleep? None. We all want conscious existence.

In sum, we want eternal, blissful, conscious existence: *Sat-Chit-Ananda* (Existence-Consciousness-Bliss). That is the Hindu name for God. But for a pragmatical consideration only, we emphasize the blissful aspect of God and our motive for Bliss, leaving out the aspects of *Sat* and

Chit, that is, *conscious existence* (also other aspects of Him not dwelt on here).

What Is God?

Now, what is God? If God be something other than Bliss, and His contact produces in us no Bliss, or produces in us only pain, or if His contact does not drive pain away from us, should we want Him? No. If God is something useless to us, we want Him not. What is the use of a God who remains always unknown and whose presence is not *inwardly* manifest to us in at least some circumstances in our lives?

Whatever conception of God we form by the exercise of reason (such as: "He is transcendent" or "He is immanent") will always remain vague and indistinct unless really felt as such. In fact, we keep God at a safe distance, conceiving Him sometimes as a mere personal being, and then again *theoretically* thinking of Him as being within us.

It is because of this vagueness in our idea and experience concerning God that we are not able to grasp the real necessity for Him and the pragmatical value of religion. This colorless theory or idea fails to bring conviction to us. It does not change our lives, influence our conduct in an appreciable way, or make us try to know God.

Proof of God's Existence
Lies Within Ourselves

What does Universal Religion say about God? It says that the proof of the existence of God lies in ourselves. It is an inner experience. You can surely recall at least one moment in your life when, in prayer or worship, you felt that the trammels of your body had nearly vanished, that the duality of experience — pleasure and pain, petty love and hate, and so on — had receded from your mind. Pure Bliss and tranquillity had welled up in your heart and you enjoyed an unruffled calm — Bliss and contentment.

Though this kind of higher experience does not often come to all, yet there can be no doubt that all men, at some time or other, in prayer or in a mood of worship or meditation, have enjoyed a few moments of unalloyed peace.

Is this not a proof of the existence of God? What direct proof can we give of the existence and nature of God, other than the existence of Bliss in ourselves in real prayer or worship? Though there is the cosmological proof of the existence of God — from effect we rise to cause, from the world to the World-Maker. And there is the teleological proof as well — from the *telos* (plan, adaptation) in the world, we rise to the Supreme Intelligence that makes the plan and adaptation. There is also the moral proof — from conscience and the sense

Sri Sri Paramahansa Yogananda with a few of the delegates to the International Congress of Religious Liberals, October 1920, Boston, Massachusetts. Sri Sri Yogananda spoke to the distinguished assemblage on "The Science of Religion"

Unity House, scene of International Congress of Religious Liberals

Sri Sri Paramahansa Yogananda speaking in Denver, Colorado, August 1924

of perfection we rise to the Perfect Being to whom our responsibility is due.

Still, we should admit that these proofs are more or less the products of inference. We cannot have full or direct knowledge of God through the limited powers of the intellect. Intellect gives only a partial and indirect view of things. To view a thing intellectually is not to see it by being one with it: it is to view a thing by being apart from it. But intuition, which we shall later explain, is the direct grasp of truth. It is in this intuition that Bliss-consciousness, or God-consciousness, is realized.

There is not a shadow of doubt as to the absolute identity of Bliss-consciousness and God-consciousness, because when we have that Bliss-consciousness we feel that our narrow individuality has been transformed and that we have risen above the duality of petty love and hate, pleasure and pain, and have attained a level from which the painfulness and worthlessness of ordinary consciousness become glaringly apparent.

And we also feel an inward expansion and all-embracing sympathy for all things. The tumults of the world die away, excitements disappear, and the "all in One and One in all" consciousness seems to dawn upon us. A glorious vision of light appears. All imperfections, all angularities, sink into nothingness. We seem to be translated into another region, the fountainhead of perennial Bliss, the starting point of one unending continuity. Is

not Bliss-consciousness, then, the same as God-consciousness, in which the above states of realization
appear?

It is evident, therefore, that God cannot be better conceived than as Bliss if we try to bring Him within the
range of everyone's calm experience. No longer will God
be a supposition then, to be theorized over. Is this not a
nobler conception of God? He is perceived as manifesting Himself in our hearts in the form of Bliss in
meditation — in prayerful or worshipful mood.

Religion Is Made Universally Necessary
Only When God Is Conceived as Bliss

If we conceive of God in this way, as Bliss, then and
then only may we make religion universally necessary.
For no one can deny that he wishes to attain Bliss and, if
he wishes to achieve it in the proper way, he is going to be
religious through approaching and feeling God, who is
described as very close to his heart as Bliss.

This Bliss-consciousness or God-consciousness can
pervade all our actions and moods, if we but let it. If we
can get a firm hold on this, we shall be able to judge the
relative religious worth of man's every action and motive
on this earth.

If we are once convinced that the attainment of this
Bliss-consciousness is our religion, our goal, our ultimate
end, then all doubts as to the meaning of multifarious

teachings, injunctions, and prohibitions of the different faiths of the world will disappear. Everything will be interpreted in the light of the stage of growth for which it is prescribed.

Truth will shine out, the mystery of existence will be solved, and a light will be thrown upon the details of our lives, with their various actions and motives. We shall be able to separate the naked truth from the outward appendages of religious doctrines and to see the worthlessness of the conventions that so often mislead people and create differences between them.

Furthermore, if religion is understood in this way, there is no man in the world — whether boy, youth, or old person — who cannot practice it, whatever may be the station of life to which he belongs, whether that of student, laborer, lawyer, doctor, carpenter, scholar, or philanthropist. If to abolish the sense of want and attain Bliss is religion, who is there that is not trying to be religious and that will not try to be so in a greater degree, if proper methods are pointed out to him?

Herein does not arise the question of the variety of religions — that of Christ, Mohammed, or of Sri Krishna. Everyone in the world is inevitably trying to be religious, and can seek to be more completely so by the adoption of proper means. There is no distinction here of caste or creed, sect or faith, dress or clime, age or sex, profession or position. For this religion is universal.

If you said that all the people of the world ought to acknowledge Sri Krishna as their Savior, would all the Christians and the Mohammedans accept that? If you asked everyone to take Jesus as their Lord, would all the Hindus and Mohammedans do that? And if you bade all to accept Mohammed as their Prophet, would the Christians and Hindus agree to that?

But if you say, "Oh, my Christian, Mohammedan, and Hindu brethren, your Lord God is Ever-Blissful Conscious Existence (Being)," will they not accept this? Can they possibly reject it? Will they not demand Him as the only One who can put an end to all their miseries?

Nor may one escape this conclusion by saying that Christians, Hindus, and Mohammedans do not conceive Jesus, Krishna, and Mohammed respectively as the Lord God — they are thought to be only the standard-bearers of God, the human incarnations of divinity. What if one does think that way? It is not the physical bodies of Jesus, Krishna, and Mohammed that we are primarily interested in, nor are we so much concerned with the historical place they occupy.

Nor are they solely memorable to us because of their different and interesting ways of preaching truth. *We revere them because they knew and felt God.* It is that fact which interests us in their historical existence and in their manifold ways of expressing the truth.

Did not all of them realize God as Bliss and reveal real

blessedness as true godliness? Is not that a sufficient bond of unity among them—let alone other aspects of Godhead and truth they may have realized and expressed? Should not a Christian, a Hindu, and a Mohammedan find interest in one another's prophets, inasmuch as all of them attained God-consciousness? As God unites all religions, it is the realization of Him as Bliss that unites the consciousness of the prophets of all religions.*

In God or Bliss-Consciousness
Our Spiritual Aspirations Find Fulfillment

One should not think that this conception of God is too abstract, having nothing to do with our spiritual hopes and aspirations, which require the conception of God as a personal being. It is not the conception of an impersonal being, as commonly understood, nor that of a personal being, as narrowly conceived.

God is not a person, as are we in our narrowness. Our being, consciousness, feeling, volition have but a shadow of resemblance to His Being (Existence),

* Bliss-consciousness is also stressed in so-called atheistic religions, such as Buddhism. The Buddhistic *Nirvana* is not, as mistakenly supposed by many Western writers, a "blowing out of light," an extinction of existence. It is rather the stage where narrow individuality is blotted out and transcendent calm in universality is reached. This is exactly what comes in higher Bliss -consciousness, though the name of God is not attached to it by the Buddhist.

Consciousness, and Bliss. He is a person in the transcendental sense. Our being, consciousness, and feeling
are limited and empirical; His, unlimited and transcendental. He has an impersonal and absolute aspect, but
we should not think He is beyond the reach of all experience — even our inner one.

He comes within the calm experience of all. It is in
Bliss-consciousness that we realize Him. There can be no
other direct proof of His existence. It is in Him as Bliss
that our spiritual hopes and aspirations find fulfillment,
our devotion and love find an object.

A conception of a personal being who is nothing but
ourselves magnified is not required. God may be or
become anything — personal, impersonal, all-merciful,
omnipotent, and so forth. But we are not required to take
note of these. Whatever conception we have put forth
exactly suits our purposes, our hopes, our aspirations,
and our perfection.

Nor should we think that this conception of God will
make us dreamy idealists, severing our connection with
the duties and responsibilities, joys and sorrows, of the
practical world. If God is Bliss and if we seek Bliss to
know Him, we may not neglect the duties and responsibilities of the world. In the performance of them we can
still feel Bliss, for it is beyond them, and so they cannot
affect it. We transcend the joys and sorrows of the world
in Bliss, but we do not transcend the necessity of

performing our rightful duties in the world.

The man of Self-realization knows that God is the Doer; all power to perform actions flows into us from Him. He that is centered in his spiritual Self feels himself to be the dispassionate seer of all actions — whether he is seeing, hearing, feeling, smelling, tasting, or undergoing various other experiences on earth. Immersed in Bliss, such men live their lives in accordance with God's will.

When nonattachment is cultivated, narrow egoism vanishes. We feel that we are playing our appointed parts on the stage of the world, without being inwardly affected by the weal and woe, love and hate, that the playing of a part involves.

The Great Play of Life

Verily, in all respects the world may be likened to a stage. The stage manager chooses people to help him in the enactment of a certain play. He allots particular parts to particular persons; all of them work according to his directions. One the stage manager makes a king, one a minister, one a servant, another the hero, and so on. One person has to play a sorrowful part, another a joyful role.

If each man plays his part according to the directions of the stage manager, then the play, with all its diversities of comical, serious, sorrowful parts, becomes successful. Even the insignificant parts have their indispensable places in the play.

The success of the play lies in the perfect acting out of each part. Each actor plays his role of sorrow or pleasure realistically, and to all outward appearances seems to be affected by it; but inwardly he remains untouched by it or by the passions he portrays — love, hate, desire, malice, pride, humility.

But if an actor, in the playing of a part, identified himself with a certain situation or a particular feeling expressed in the play and lost his own individuality, he would be thought foolish, to say the least. A story will bring out the latter point clearly.

Once in the house of a rich man the play of *Ramayana** was staged. In the course of the play it was found that the man who should play the part of Hanuman, the attendant-friend of Rama† was missing. In his perplexity the stage manager seized upon an ugly simpleton, Nilkamal by name, and sought to make him enact the part of Hanuman.

Nilkamal at first refused, but was forced to appear on the stage. His ugly appearance excited loud laughter among the spectators and they began to shout in merriment, "Hanuman, Hanuman!"

Nilkamal could hardly bear this. He forgot that it was only a play, and bawled out in exasperation, "Why, sirs,

* A dramatization based on the ancient Sanskrit epic of the same name. *(Publisher's Note)*

† The central sacred figure of the Ramayana *(Publisher's Note)*

do you call me Hanuman? Why do you laugh? I am not a Hanuman. The stage manager made me come out here this way."

In this complex world our lives are nothing but plays. But alas, we identify ourselves with the play, and hence feel disgust, sorrow and pleasure. We forget the direction and injunction of the Great Stage Manager. In the act of living our lives — playing our parts — we feel as real all our sorrows and pleasures, loves and hates — in a word, we become attached, affected.

This play of the world is without beginning and end. Everyone should play his part, as assigned by the Great Stage Manager, ungrudgingly; should play for the sake of the play only; should act sorrowful when playing sorrowful parts, or pleased when playing pleasurable parts, but should never be inwardly identified with the play.

Nor should one wish to play another's part. If everyone in the world portrayed the role of a king, the play itself would lose interest and meaning.

He that has attained Bliss-consciousness will *feel* the world to be a stage and will play out his part as best he can, remembering the Great Stage Manager, God, and knowing and feeling His plan and direction.

Part 4

Four Fundamental Religious Methods

The Need for Religious Methods

We have seen in Parts 1, 2, and 3 that the identification of the spiritual Self with body and mind is the fundamental cause of our pain, suffering, and limitations; and that because of this identification we feel such excitations as pain and pleasure, and are almost blind to the state of Bliss, or God-consciousness. We have also seen that religion essentially consists in the permanent avoidance of such pain and in the attainment of pure Bliss, or God.

As the sun's true image cannot be perceived in the surface of moving water, so the true blissful nature of the spiritual Self—the reflection of the Universal Spirit—cannot be understood, owing to the waves of disquietude that arise from identification of the self with the changing states of the body and mind. As the moving waters distort the true image of the sun, so does the disturbed state of the mind, through identification, distort the true, ever-blissful nature of the inner Self.

The purpose of this chapter is to discuss the easiest, most rational, and most fundamental methods — practical for all — that will free the ever-blissful spiritual Self from its baneful connection and identification with the transitory body and mind, thus causing it permanently to avoid pain and attain Bliss, which constitutes religion.

Therefore the fundamental methods to be considered are religious and involve religious actions, because only by means of these can the spiritual Self be freed from identification with the body and mind and thus from pain, and be able to attain permanent Bliss, or God.

The "Son of God" and the "Son of Man"

When Christ called himself the "Son of God," he meant the Universal Spirit dwelling in him. In John 10:36 Jesus says: "Of him whom the Father hath sanctified and sent into the world … I said, I am the Son of God."

But, at other times, when Christ used another phrase — the "Son of man" — he meant the physical body, the offspring of man, the flesh that is born out of another human body. For instance, in Matthew 20:18-19, Jesus says to the disciples: "Behold, we go up to Jerusalem; and the Son of man shall be betrayed unto the chief priests … and they shall … deliver him to the Gentiles … to crucify him."

In John 3:5-6, Christ says: "Except a man be born of water (the oceanic vibration of *Aum* or *Amen,* the Holy

Ghost, the Invisible Force that upholds all creation; God in His immanent aspect of the Creator) and of the Spirit, he cannot enter into the kingdom of God. That which is born of the flesh is flesh; and that which is born of the Spirit is Spirit." These words mean that unless we can *transcend* the body and realize ourselves as Spirit, we cannot enter into the kingdom or state of that Universal Spirit.

This thought is echoed in a Sanskrit couplet of the Hindu scriptures: "If thou canst transcend the body and perceive thyself as Spirit, thou shalt be eternally blissful, free from all pain."

Now, there are *four* fundamental, universal religious methods which, if followed in daily life, will in time liberate the spiritual Self from the trammels of its bodily and mental vehicles. Under these four classes of religious methods I include all the possible religious practices that have ever been enjoined by any saint or savant or prophet of God.

The Origin of Sectarianism

Religious practices are inculcated by prophets in the form of doctrines. Men of limited intellect, failing to interpret the true import of these doctrines, accept their exoteric or outer meaning and gradually fall into forms, conventions, and rigid practices. This is the origin of sectarianism.

Rest from work on the sabbath day was wrongly

interpreted to mean rest from all work—even religious work. This is the danger to men of limited understanding. We should remember that we are not made for the sabbath, but that the sabbath is made for us; we are not made for rules, rules are made for us—they change as we change. We are to hold to the essence of a rule, not dogmatically to its form.

Change of forms and customs constitutes for many a change from one religion to another. Nevertheless, the deepest import of all the doctrines of all the different prophets is essentially the same. Most men do not understand this.

There is equal danger in the case of the intellectually great: They try to know the Highest Truth by the exercise of the intellect alone; but the Highest Truth can be known only by realization. Realization is something other than mere understanding. We could not possibly understand intellectually the sweetness of sugar if we had not tasted it. Just so, religious knowledge is drawn from the deepest experience of one's own soul. This we often forget when we seek to learn about God, religious dogmas, and morality. We seldom seek to know these through inner religious experience.

It is a pity that men of great intellectual power, successful in their use of reason in the way of discovering the deep truths of the natural sciences and other fields of knowledge, think that they will also be able to grasp intellectually the highest religious and moral truths. It is also a pity that the intellect or reason of these men, instead of being a help, is often found to be a bar to their comprehension of the Highest Truth by the only means possible — living it in one's life.

Let us consider the four methods characterizing religious growth.

FOUR FUNDAMENTAL RELIGIOUS METHODS

1. The Intellectual Method

The intellectual method is the commonly adopted natural method, not quickly effective in realizing the end.

Intellectual development and progression has been natural and hence common to all rational beings. It is our self-conscious understanding that differentiates us from the lower animals, which are conscious but not self-conscious.

In the grades and processes of evolution, we see that this consciousness gradually becomes self-consciousness — from animal consciousness self-consciousness arises. The consciousness gradually tries to free itself and tries to know itself by itself; thus it is changed into self-consciousness. This change is due to an evolutional necessity, and the universal urge toward intellectual pursuits is due to this evolutional tendency. The spiritual Self, identified with various degrees and sorts of bodily

and mental states, tries gradually and naturally to return
to itself through itself.

The development of the conscious thought-process is
one of the methods that the spiritual Self adopts to rise
above the trammels of the body and mind. The effort of
the spiritual Self to return to itself — its lost condition —
through development of the thought-process is natural.
This is the process of the world.

The Universal Spirit expresses itself in different grades
of development, from lower to higher. In stone and earth
there is no life or consciousness as we can conceive it. In
trees there is vegetative growth, an approach to life, yet
no unhampered life and no conscious thought-process at
all. In animals there is life and also consciousness of life.
In man — the culmination point — there is life, consciousness of it, and also consciousness of the Self
(Self-consciousness).

Hence it is natural for man to develop himself through
thinking and reasoning, by deep study of books, by original research work, and by laborious investigations into
causes and effects in the natural world.

The more deeply man engages in thought-processes,
the more he may be said to be utilizing the "method" by
which he has come to be what he is in the course of the
world-evolution process (that is, the method by which
consciousness develops into Self-consciousness) and the
nearer, knowingly or unknowingly, he approaches the

Self—for *in thought we rise above the body.*

The deliberate following of this method will bring about sure results. Exercise of thought in study, for the acquirement of knowledge in a particular field, though to some extent improving the Self-consciousness, is not so effective as that thought-process which has as its sole object the transcending of the body and seeing the truth.

In India, the intellectual method in its highest form is called *Jnana Yoga*—the attainment of true wisdom through recollectedness and discrimination, such as constantly reminding oneself: "I am not the body. The passing show of creation cannot affect my Self. I am Spirit."

One of the defects of this method is that it is a very *slow* process for the spiritual Self to thus realize itself. It may involve a good deal of time. While the spiritual Self begins to apprehend Self-consciousness by this method, still it is always engaged in a series of passing mental thoughts with which it has no relation.

Tranquillity of the Spirit is something beyond thought and bodily sensation, though when once attained it overflows into them.

2. The Devotional Method

This consists in the attempt to fix our attention on one object of thought, rather than on different series of thoughts and on various subjects (as in the intellectual method).

Sri Sri Paramahansa Yogananda in New York, 1926

One of the first meetings conducted by Sri Sri
Paramahansa Yogananda at the SRF international
headquarters in Los Angeles, 1925

Yogoda Satsanga Society of India Administration
Building, Branch Math and Ashram, Ranchi

Under the devotional method are included all forms of worship, such as prayer (from which we should eliminate all thoughts of worldly things). The spiritual Self should fix its attention deeply and reverently on whatever it chooses to concentrate on — whether the thought of a personal God or of an impersonal Omnipresence. The main point is that the devotee should concentrate on one devotional thought *in good earnest.*

By this process the spiritual Self becomes gradually freed from the disturbances of many thoughts — the second series of disturbances — and gets time and opportunity to think of itself in itself. When we pray earnestly, we forget all bodily sensations and drive away all intruding thoughts that try to engage our attention.

The deeper our prayer, the more intense is the satisfaction felt, and this becomes the criterion by which we measure how far we have approached Bliss-God. As the bodily sensations are left behind and as the vagrant thoughts are checked, the superiority of this over the foregoing method becomes manifest.

However, this method presents certain defects and difficulties. Owing to the long-continued attachment and slavery of the spiritual Self to the body — to this deep-rooted bad habit — it ineffectually tries to turn its attention away from the sphere of bodily and mental sensations.

However much one may wish to pray or engage in any form of worship with one's whole heart, one's attention is

mercilessly invaded by the raiding bodily sensations and
fleeting thoughts brought in by memory. In prayer we are
often wholly engrossed in the consideration of the circumstances favorable to it, or we are too ready to remove
any of our disturbing bodily discomforts.

In spite of all our conscious efforts, our bad habit,
which has become a second nature to us, lords it over the
Self's wishes. In spite of our desire, the mind becomes
restless, and, to paraphrase, "Wherever your mind shall
be there shall your heart be also." We are told to pray to
God with all our hearts. Instead, we generally pray while
our minds and hearts are distracted by roving thoughts
and sensory impressions.

3. The Meditational Method

This and the next method are purely scientific, involv-
ing a practical course of training, and are prescribed by
great sages who personally have realized the truth in their
own lives. I myself learned from one of these.

There is nothing of mystery in these methods, nor anything to be dreaded as harmful; they are easy, if one is
properly acquainted with them. They will be found to be
universally true. Practically felt knowledge is the best
proof of their validity and pragmatic utility.

By undergoing regularly the processes of meditation
till they become a habit, we can bring upon ourselves a
state of "conscious sleep." We generally experience this

calm and pleasurable tranquil state just when we are falling into deep sleep and approaching unconsciousness, or rising from it and approaching consciousness.

In this state of conscious sleep we become free from all thoughts and outer bodily sensations, and the Self gets opportunity to think of itself—it comes into the blissful state from time to time, according to the depth and frequency of its practice of meditation.

In this state we are temporarily forgetful of and free from all bodily and mental disturbances which divert the Self's attention. By this process of meditation the outer or sensory organs are controlled by the quieting of the voluntary nerves, as in sleep.

This state of meditation is the first and not the final state of real meditation. In conscious sleep we learn to control only the outer or sensory organs; the only difference being that in ordinary sleep the sensory organs are automatically controlled, while in meditation the sensory organs are voluntarily controlled.

However, in this early stage of meditation the spiritual Self is still liable to disturbance by the involuntary and internal organs; for example, the lungs, heart, and other parts of the body that we mistakenly suppose to be beyond control.*

* We seldom learn, as great saints and savants have learned, how to give rest to these internal organs. Because we suppose them to be beyond control, they get overworked and suddenly stop, which stoppage we term "death" or the "great sleep".

We must look for a better method than this; for so long as the spiritual Self cannot at will shut out all bodily sensations — even interior ones, which are the occasions of the rise of thoughts — but remains vulnerable to these disturbances, it can have no hope of control nor of time or opportunity to know itself.

4. The Scientific Method or Yoga

St. Paul said: *"I die daily."** By this he meant that he knew the process of controlling the internal organs and could voluntarily free his spiritual Self from the body and mind — an experience that ordinary untrained people only feel at final death, when the spiritual Self is freed from the worn-out body.

Now, by undergoing a practical and regular course of training in this scientific method,† the Self can be felt as being separate from the body, *without final death.*

I will give only a general idea of the process and the true scientific theory on which it is based. I set it down here from my own experience. I may say it will be found to be universally true. And I may also safely say that Bliss, which is, as I pointed out, our ultimate end, is felt in an

---

* Corinthians 15:31.

† The scientific method referred to here and throughout the remainder of the book is *Kriya Yoga,* an ancient spiritual science that includes certain yogic techniques of meditation taught by Paramahansa Yogananda in the *Yogoda Satsanga Lessons. (Publisher's Note)*

intense degree in the act of practicing this method. The practice of it is itself intensely blissful —far more purely blissful, I venture to say, than the greatest enjoyment that any of our five senses or the mind can ever afford us.

I do not wish to give anyone any other proof of its truth than is afforded by his own experience. The more one practices it with patience and regularity, the more one feels intensely and durably fixed in Bliss.

Owing to the persistence of bad habits, the consciousness of bodily existence — with all its memories — revives occasionally and fights against that tranquillity. But if anyone practices regularly and for extended periods, it may be guaranteed that in time he will find himself in a highly supramental state of Bliss.

We should not, however, over-wisely seek to imagine beforehand the possible results to which the process may lead, and then cease practicing the method after a short trial. In order to make real progress, the following are necessary: first, loving attention to the subject to be learned; second, desire to learn and an earnest spirit of inquiry; third, steadfastness until the desired end is attained.

If we go only half way and then, after a short practice, reject it, the desired result will not follow. A novice in spiritual practices who tries to prejudge the experience of experts (the masters and prophets of all ages) is like a child that attempts to imagine what post-graduate courses would be like.

It is a great pity that people will spend their best efforts and time in securing what is needed for worldly existence or indulging in intellectual controversy over theories, but seldom seem to think it worth their while to realize and patiently experience in life the truths which not only vivify but impart meaning to it. Misguided efforts often engage their attention longer than well-guided efforts.

I have been practicing the above-mentioned method for many years, and the more I do so, the more I feel the joy of a state of permanent and unfailing Bliss.

We should bear in mind that the spiritual Self has been in bondage to the body for how many ages we know not. It may not be freed in one day, nor will short or desultory practice of the method take one to the supreme state of Bliss or give one control over the internal organs. It may require patient practice for a long, long time.

This can be guaranteed, however, that the following of this process will bring the great joy of pure Bliss-con-sciousness. The more we practice it, the more quickly we attain Bliss. I wish that, as seekers of Bliss, which all of us are, you would try to experience for yourselves that uni-versal truth which is in all and may be felt by all. This state is not an invention of anyone. It is already there; we have simply to discover it.

Do not, until you have tested this truth, look upon what I write with indifference. It may be that you are tired of hearing various theories, none of which has hitherto had any direct bearing on your life. This is no theory, but realized truth. I am trying to give you an idea of what can be really experienced.

I had the good fortune to learn this holy, scientific truth from a great saint* of India many years ago. You may ask why I urge you — why I draw your attention to these facts. Have I any selfish interest? To this I answer in the affirmative. I wish to give this truth to you with the hope of getting in return pure joy for having helped you to find your joy in the practice and realization of it.

Physiological Explanation of the Scientific Method

Now I have to enter into a little physiology, which will enable us to understand the method, at least in a general way. I will refer to the work of the main centers and to the electrical current that flows from the brain through these centers to the outer (sensory) and internal organs, keeping them vibrating with life.

There are six main centers through which pranic current (vital current or life electricity)† from the brain is

---

* Swami Sri Yukteswar, guru of Paramahansa Yogananda. *(Publisher's Note)*

† The intelligent, finer-than-atomic energy (*prana* or life-force) that activates and sustains life in the body. *(Publisher's Note)*

discharged throughout the nervous system. These are:

1. Medulla center	4. Lumbar center
2. Cervical center	5. Sacral center
3. Dorsal center	6. Coccygeal center

The brain is the supreme electrical power-house (highest center). All the centers are connected with one another and act under the influence of the supreme center (brain cells). The brain cells discharge life current, or electricity, through these centers, which in turn discharge electricity to the different efferent and afferent nerves, which respectively carry motor impulses and sensations of touch, sight, and so forth.

This electrical flow from the brain is the life of the organism (of its internal and external organs), and it is this electrical medium through which all our sensory reports reach the brain and cause thought reactions.

The Self, if it wishes to shut out effectively the disturbing reports of bodily sensations (which are also the occasions of the rise of the thought-series), must control and concentrate the electrical flow and draw it back from the nervous system as a whole to the seven main centers (including the brain), so that by this process it may give the outer and internal organs perfect rest.

In sleep, the electrical conductivity between the brain and the sensory organs is partially inhibited, so that ordinary sensations of sound, touch, and so forth, do not reach the brain. But because this inhibition is not complete, a sufficiently strong stimulus from without restores this electrical conductivity and is reported to the brain, awakening the person. Yet always in sleep there is a steady electrical flow into the internal organs—heart, lungs, and other parts—so that they keep on throbbing and working.

Practice of Scientific Method Results in Freedom from Bodily and Mental Distractions

As the control of life electricity in sleep is not complete, bodily sensations of discomfort, disease, or strong outside stimuli disturb it. But through a scientific process of control, which may not here be described in detail, we can control simultaneously the external and the internal organs of the system in a perfect way. That is the ultimate result of practice. But it may take long years to attain that perfect control.

As after sleep (which is rest) the outer organs are invigorated, so, after the rest resulting from practice of this scientific method, the internal organs are greatly vitalized; and with the consequent increase in their working power, life is prolonged.

As we do not fear to go to sleep lest for the time being the sensory organs remain inert, so we ought not to fear to practice conscious death, that is, give rest to the internal organs. Death will then be under our control; for when we think this bodily house is unfit and broken, we shall be able to leave it of our own accord. "The last enemy that shall be destroyed is death."*

We may describe the process thus: If the main telephone office in a town is permanently connected by wires with different parts of the town, people telephoning from those parts can always, even against the will of the authorities of the main telephone office, send messages to the central office through the medium of the electric current running along the connecting wires. If the main telephone office wishes to stop communication with the different parts, it can turn off the main electrical switch and there will be no flow to the different quarters of the town.

Similarly, the scientific method teaches a process enabling us to draw to our *central part*—spine and brain —the life current distributed throughout the organs and other parts of our body. The process consists of magnetizing the spinal column and the brain, which contain the seven main centers, with the result that the distributed life electricity is drawn back to the original centers of discharge and is experienced in the form of light. In this state the spiritual Self can consciously free itself from its bodily and mental distractions.

The spiritual Self is, as it were, being disturbed, even against its wish, by the telephone reports from two classes of people—gentlemen (thoughts) and lower-class people

* I Corinthians 15:26.

(bodily sensations). In order to break connection with them, the Self has only to draw away the electricity flowing through the telephone wires to the central battery of its house by turning off the switch (practicing the fourth method), in order to enjoy relief.

Attention is the great director and discharger of energy. It is the active cause of the discharge of the electrical life current from the brain to the sensory and motor nerves. For example, we drive away a troublesome fly by discharging, through the power of attention, electrical current along the motor nerves, thereby producing the desired movement of the hand. I cite this to give an idea of the power by which the electrical flow of the system can be controlled and drawn back to its seven centers.

It is these seven starlike (astral) cerebrospinal centers and their mystery that are mentioned in Revelation in the Bible. St. John unsealed the hidden openings of the seven centers and ascended to true understanding of himself as Spirit. "Write the things which thou hast seen ... the mystery of the seven stars."*

Continued Practice of Scientific Method
Leads to Bliss-Consciousness, or God

In conclusion I wish to describe the nature of the states which emerge when the electrical flow is

---

* Revelation 1:19, 20.

completely controlled. In the beginning a most attractive sensation is felt in the course of magnetizing the spinal column. But continued and long practice will bring about a state of conscious Bliss, which counteracts the excited state produced by our body consciousness.

This blissful state has been described as our universal aim and highest necessity, because in it we are really conscious of God, or Bliss, and feel the expansion of our real selves. The more frequently this is experienced, the more our narrow individuality falls away, the sooner the state of universality is reached, and the closer and more direct is our communion with God.

Religion is really nothing but the merging of our individuality in universality. Therefore in the consciousness of this blissful state we ascend the steps of religion. We leave the noxious atmosphere of the senses and vagrant thoughts and come to a region of heavenly Bliss.

We learn by this process what will be found to be universally true: When, by constant practice, the consciousness of this blissful state of the spiritual Self becomes real, we find ourselves always in the holy presence of the blissful God in us. We discharge our duties better, having an eye more for the duties themselves than for our egoism and the consciousness of pleasure and pain arising therefrom. Then we can solve the mystery of existence and impart real meaning to life.

In the teachings of all religions, whether it be

Christianity, Mohammedanism, or Hinduism, one truth is stressed: Until man knows himself as Spirit—the fountainhead of Bliss—he is limited by mortal concepts and subject to the inexorable laws of nature. Knowledge of his true being brings him eternal freedom.

We can know God only by knowing ourselves, for our real nature is similar to His. Man has been created in the image of God. If the methods here suggested are learned and earnestly practiced, you will know yourself to be a blissful spirit and will realize God.

The methods given in this book embrace all the conceivable means essential to the realization of God. They do leave out of consideration the thousand and one conventional rules and minor practices enjoined by the so-called different religions, because some of these relate to differences in the frame of mind of the individuals, hence are less important, though by no means unnecessary; and because others come up in the course of practice of these methods, hence do not require fuller treatment in the limited space here.

Scientific Method Works Directly With the Life-Force

The superiority of this method over others lies in the fact that it works with the exact thing that binds us down to our narrow individuality—the *life-force.* Instead of being turned back and absorbed into the expansive self-conscious force of the Self, the life-force generally goes outward, keeping the body and mind always in motion, and causing disturbances to the spiritual Self in the shape of bodily sensations and passing thoughts.

Because the life-force moves outward, sensations and thoughts disturb and distort the calm image of the Self or Soul. This method teaches us to turn the life-force inward. Hence it is *direct* and *immediate*. It takes us straight to the consciousness of Self—the Bliss-God. It does not require the help of an intermediary.

This method is to control and direct the course of the life-force by the control and regulation of a known and directly connected manifestation of the life-force itself. The other methods employ the help of the intellect, or thought process, to control the life-force in order to induce consciousness of the Self in its blissful and other aspects.

It should be noted that all religious methods in the world directly or indirectly, tacitly or expressly, enjoin the control, regulation, and turning back of the life-force so that we may transcend the body and mind and know the Self in its native state. The fourth method directly controls life-force by life-force, whereas the other methods do it indirectly through some other intermediary—thought, prayer, good works, worship, or "conscious sleep."

Presence of life in man is existence; absence of it is death. Hence the method that teaches life's direct power to control itself must be the best of all.

Savants of different ages and climes have suggested methods adapted to the mental frame and condition of the people among whom they lived and preached. Some have laid stress on prayer, some on feeling, some on good works, some on love, some on reason or thought, some on meditation. But their motives have been the same.

They all meant that body consciousness should be transcended by the turning back of the life-force inward, and that the Self should be realized, as the image of the sun appears in calm, unruffled water. Their purpose is the inculcation of just that which the fourth method teaches directly, without the help of any intermediary.

At the same time it should be noted that the practice of this method does not prevent the cultivation of the intellect, the building up of the physique, and the activity of a social and useful life — a life of the best feelings and motives, devoted to philanthropic works. As a matter of fact, *all-sided* training should be prescribed for all. It positively helps rather than retards the practice of the method; the only thing required is that its point of view be retained. Then all actions, all pursuits, will result to one's advantage.

The main thing in this process is to understand thoroughly the mystery of the life-force that sustains the bodily organism of man, causing it to vibrate with life and energy.

PART 5

Instruments of Knowledge and the Theoretical Validity of Religious Methods

The universality and necessity of the religious ideal (ever-existent, ever-conscious Bliss-God) and the practical methods to reach it have been discussed in the previous chapters. Now we wish to discuss the validity of the methods.

The methods are essentially practical, and if they are followed the ideal must be reached, whether we deal with the theories or not. Their validity is shown by the practical result itself, which is palpable and real.

It is not, be it understood, really necessary to show the theoretical grounds of validity. But simply to satisfy others we treat *a priori* of the validity of the theories of knowledge on which the methods are based, that their validity may also be theoretically shown.

This will launch us into the epistemological question: How and how far can we know the ideal, the truth? To show how we know the ideal we must consider how we know the actual world. We must deal with the process of knowing the world. Then we shall see whether the process of knowing the world is the same as the process of knowing the ideal, and whether the actual world is separate from the ideal or whether the latter pervades the former — only the process of knowing the two being different.

Before proceeding further, let us discuss the "instruments" of knowledge — the way by which knowledge of the world is made possible to us. There are three instruments or means of knowledge: perception, inference, and intuition.

THREE INSTRUMENTS OF KNOWLEDGE

1. Perception

Our senses are, as it were, windows, through which stimuli from the outside come and strike the mind, which passively receives these impressions. Unless the mind operates, no impression can be made on it by the stimuli coming from the outside through the sense-windows.

Mind not only furnishes the connections to the stimuli received through the different senses, but stores their influences in the form of impressions. However, these impressions remain a confused, disconnected mass until the discriminative faculty *(buddhi)* operates on them. A relevant connection is then established and the details of the outer world are recognized as such. They are projected, so to speak, and known in the forms of time and space, having distinct associations — quantity, quality, measure, and meaning. A house is then known as a house, and not as a post. This is the result of the operation of the intellect *(buddhi).*

We may see an object, feel it, and then hear the sound of it when struck, our mind receiving these impressions and storing them. *Buddhi* interprets them and seems to project them in the form of a house with its various parts — size, shape, color, form, fashion, and its relation to others in the present, past or future — in time and space. This is the way that knowledge of the world arises.

An insane person has impressions stored in his mind, but they are in a chaotic state — not sorted and made up into distinct, well-ordered groups by the intellect.

Now comes the question: Can Reality (the ideal, ever-conscious, ever-existent Bliss-God)be known by perception of this sort? Is the process of knowing this world (by perception) valid in the matter of knowing the highest truth?

We know that the intellect can work only upon the materials supplied by the senses. It is certain that the senses give us only the stimuli of qualities and variety. Not only do the senses give variety, but intellect itself deals with variety and remains in the region of variety. Though it can think of "unity in diversity," it cannot be one with it. This is its drawback. Intellectual perception cannot really give the true nature of the one Universal

Substance underlying diverse manifestations.

This is the verdict of reason itself. When *buddhi* turns back upon itself to judge how far it is capable of knowing Reality by interpreting the sense-impressions, it finds itself hopelessly confined within the domain of the sense-world. There is no loophole through which it can peep into the super-sensuous world.

Some may say that because we drive a wedge between the sensuous and the super-sensuous worlds, reason cannot bring itself to believe that it may have any knowledge of the super-sensuous. They say that if we think of the super-sensuous as manifesting in and through the sensuous, then in knowing the sensuous—with its connection (teleology, or adaptation) and all the details and varieties by the process of the intellect—we shall be knowing the super-sensuous manifested as "unity in diversity."

But it may be questioned, what is the nature of this "knowing"? Is it merely an idea in the brain, or is it *seeing* the truth (unity in diversity) face to face, first-hand and direct? Does this form of knowing carry the same conviction that being one with it would carry? Surely not, for this knowing is only partial, defective; it is merely looking through a colored glass. The super-sensuous world lies beyond. These are the *a priori* arguments against perception as an instrument for knowing Reality, or God.

From calm experience, also, we find that we cannot attain that blissful state, which is Reality and the ideal itself (as shown in the previous chapters), until we rise to a considerable extent from the restless, perceptual stage. The more we leave behind the disturbing perceptions and interior thoughts, the greater is the possibility of the dawning of that supramental state of Bliss, or Bliss-God.

Ordinary perception and Bliss seem to be mutually exclusive in common experience. However, none of our methods is based on pure perception, hence the inability of the latter to know Reality is not important.

2. Inference

This is another way of deriving knowledge of the world. But inference itself is based on experience — on perception — be it deductive or inductive. In our experience we find fire wherever there is smoke; hence if we see smoke on any occasion, we infer there is fire. This is deductive inference. But it is possible only because of our previous experience (perception) of smoke as being associated with fire. In inductive inference, also, there is the same dependence on perception.

We observe that a certain kind of bacillus is the cause of cholera. We find out the causal connection between that kind of bacillus and cholera and at once inductively infer that wherever we find this bacillus, cholera will be present. While there is a leap here from the known cases of cholera to the unknown cases, still by inference we get no new fact, though the cases may be new. The very possibility of the establishment of a causal connection between certain bacilli and cholera depended upon observation (perception) of specific cases.

So inference ultimately depends upon perception. In inferred cases we do not get any new truth — nothing really new that was not found in observed cases. In observed cases bacilli are followed by cholera; and in the inferred cases, too, bacilli are followed by cholera — no new truth, though the cases are fresh and new.

No matter what forms of thought, reasoning, inference, or imagination we employ, we are still not face to face with Reality. Reason or thought may arrange and systematize facts of experience; it can endeavor to see things as a whole; it may try to penetrate into the mystery of the world. But its effort is hampered by the materials on which it works — facts of experience, sense impressions. They are bald, hard facts, disconnected, limited by our powers of perception. The materials disturb rather than help the thought process, which itself has a restless continuity.

The first religious method, as we pointed out, is the intellectual method, which utilizes the thought process in order to know Reality — the state of Bliss and calm realization. But it fails. Bodily perceptions disturb us; the thought process, also, owing to its working on varied, restless sense-impressions, forbids our remaining for long in a concentrated state. We therefore fail to attain the consciousness of unity in diversity. One merit of the intellectual method is that when we are absorbed in the thought-world, to a certain extent we transcend bodily sensations. But this is always temporary.

In the other two methods — devotional and meditational — the thought process is less; still, it is present. In the devotional method (that is, in ritual or ceremonial worship, in prayer — congregational or individual) much of the thought process is engaged in the arrangement of favorable conditions. Still, there is the attempt to concentrate on some subject of worship or prayer.

So far as the diversity in thought processes is checked or prevented, the devotional method is successful. The defect is this: Owing to a bad habit, confirmed in the course of ages, our concentration is not deep, leaving the possibility of setting the diversity of thought processes to work at the slightest disturbance.

In the meditational method (outward formalities, conventions, rites being dispensed with, thus barring the possibility of the thought processes being set into motion as easily as in the devotional method) concentration is fixed on one object of thought. There is then a gradual tendency to leave the sphere of thought behind and to step into the sphere of intuition, which we shall next consider.

3. Intuition

So far we have been considering the instruments and processes of knowing this sensuous world. Intuition, with which we now deal, is the process by which we know the super-sensuous world — the world that is beyond senses and thoughts. It is true that the super-sensuous expresses itself in and through the sensuous, and to know the latter in completeness is to know the former; but the process of knowing the two must be different.

Are we able to know even the sensory world in all its fullness merely by perception and thought? Assuredly not. There is an infinite number of facts, things, laws, and connections in nature and even in our own organism that are still a sealed book to mankind. Far less, then, shall we be able to know the super-sensuous realm by perception and thought.

Intuition comes from within; thought from without. Intuition gives a face-to-face view of Reality; thought gives an indirect view of it. Intuition, by a strange sympathy, sees Reality in its totality, while thought chops it up into parts.

Every man has the power of intuition, as he has the power of thought. As thought can be cultivated, so intuition can be developed. In intuition we are in tune with Reality — with the world of Bliss, with the "unity in diversity," with the inner laws governing the spiritual world, with God.

How do we know that we exist? Through senseperception? Do the senses first tell us that we exist — whence the consciousness of existence comes? That can never be, for the consciousness of existence is presupposed in the attempt of the senses to let us know of our existence. Sense cannot consciously be aware of anything without our first knowing that we exist in the very act of sensing.

Does inference, the thought process, tell us that we exist? Assuredly not. For the materials of thought must be sense-impressions, which, as we have just found, cannot tell us of our existence, as that feeling is already presupposed in them. Nor can the process of thought give us the consciousness of existence, for the latter is already implied in the former. When, by comparing ourselves with the outer world, we endeavor to think or infer that we exist therein, the consciousness of existence is already present in the very act of thinking and inferring.

Then, if sense or thought fails, how do we know that we exist? It is only by intuition that we can know this. Such knowing is *one form* of intuition. It is beyond sense and thought — they are made possible by it.

It is very difficult to define intuition, for it is too near to every one of us; every one of us feels it. Do we not know what the consciousness of existence is? Every one knows it. It is too familiar to admit of definition. Ask one how he knows he exists; he will remain dumb. He knows it, but he cannot define it. He may try to explain, but his explanation does not reveal what he inwardly feels. Intuition of every form has this peculiar character.

The fourth religious method, explained in the last

chapter, bases itself on intuition. The more earnest we are about it, the wider and surer will be our vision of Reality — God.

It is through intuition that humanity reaches Divinity, that the sensuous is brought into connection with the super-sensuous, and that the latter is *felt* to express itself in and through the sensuous. The influence of senses vanishes; intruding thoughts disappear; Bliss-God is realized; the consciousness of "all in One and One in all" dawns upon us. This intuition is what all great savants and prophets of the world possessed.

The third, or meditational method, as explained in Part 4, also carries us into the region of intuition — when it is earnestly practiced. But it is a bit round-about, and ordinarily takes a longer time to produce in us the successive states of the intuitional or realization process.

By Intuition God Can Be Realized in All His Aspects

Thus it is by intuition that God can be realized in all His aspects. We have no sense that can reveal knowledge of Him; the senses give knowledge only of His manifestations. No thought or inference can enable us to know Him as He truly is, for thought cannot go beyond the data of the senses; it can only arrange and interpret the impressions of the senses.

When the senses are unable, thought (which depends

upon them) is also unable to bring us to God. So it is to intuition that we shall have to turn for knowledge of God in His blissful and other aspects.

However, there are many bars to this intuitional point of view—to the realization of truth. These are some of them: disease, mental incapacity, doubt, indolence, worldly-mindedness, false ideas, and instability.

These are either inherent or engendered and aggravated through association with others. Our inherent tendencies (samskaras) to certain faults may be overcome by strong-minded effort (purushakara). By exercise of will power we can remove all our short-comings. It is by right effort and by association with good people, devotees of God, that we can eradicate bad habits and form good ones. Until we associate with those who have seen, felt, and realized true religion in their lives, we may not fully know what it is, and in what its universality and necessity lie.

The spirit of inquiry is in all. Everyone in the world is a seeker after truth. It is his immortal heritage; and he seeks it, blindly or wisely, until he has fully reclaimed it. It is never too late to mend. "Seek, and ye shall find; knock and it shall be opened unto you."*

---

* Matthew 7:7.

About the Author

"The ideal of love for God and service to humanity found full expression in the life of Paramahansa Yogananda.... Though the major part of his life was spent outside India, still he takes his place among our great saints. His work continues to grow and shine ever more brightly, drawing people everywhere on the path of the pilgrimage of the Spirit."

In these words, the Government of India paid tribute to the founder of Yogoda Satsanga Society of India/Self-Realization Fellowship, upon issuing a commemorative stamp in his honour on March 7, 1977, the seventeen anniversary of his passing.

A world teacher whose presence among us illumined the path for countless souls, Paramahansa Yogananda lived and taught the highest truths of life. Born in Gorakhpur, India, in 1893, Paramahansa Yogananda was sent by his guru to the United States in 1920 as India's delegate to an International Congress of Religious Liberals. Subsequent lectures in Boston, New York, and Philadelphia were enthusiastically received, and in 1924 he embarked on a cross-continental speaking tour.

For the next decade Paramahansaji travelled extensively, giving lectures and classes in which he instructed thousands of men and women in the yoga science of meditation and balanced spiritual living.

Today, the spiritual and humanitarian work begun by Paramahansa Yogananda continues under the direction of Sri Sri Mrinalini Mata, one of his closest disciples and current president of Yogoda Satsanga Society of India/Self-Realization Fellowship. In addition to publishing Paramahansa Yogananda's writings, lectures, and informal talks (including a comprehensive series of lessons for home study),* his society oversees ashrams, kendras, and meditation centres around the world; monastic training programs; and the Worldwide Prayer Circle, which serves as a channel to help bring healing to those in need and greater peace and harmony among all nations. Seekers in India and surrounding territories are served by Yogoda Satsanga Society of India.

Quincy Howe, Jr., Ph. D., Professor of Ancient Languages, Scripps College, wrote: "Paramahansa Yogananda brought to the West not only India's perennial promise of God-realization, but also a practical method by which spiritual aspirants from all walks of life may progress rapidly toward that goal. Originally appreciated in the West only on the most lofty and abstract level, the spiritual legacy of India is now accessible as practice and experience to all who aspire to know God, not in the beyond, but in the here and now .... Yogananda has placed within the reach of all the most exalted methods of contemplation."

The life and teachings of Paramahansa Yogananda are described in his *Autobiography of a Yogi,* which has become a classic in its field since its publication in 1946 and is now used as a text and reference work in many colleges and universities throughout the world. An award-winning documentary film about Paramahansa Yogananda's life and work, *Awake: The Life of Yogananda,* was released in October 2014.

---

* These lessons present the art of spiritual living and the yoga meditation techniques tautht by Paramahansa Yogananda, including Kriya Yoga, an ancient spiritual science whose devoted practice leads to direct, personal experience of God. Information about the lessons is available from Yogoda Satsanga Society of India (See Page 84).

Sri Sri Paramahansa Yogananda: A Yogi in Life and Death

Sri Sri Paramahansa Yogananda entered *mahasamadhi* (a yogi's final conscious exit from the body) in Los Angeles, California, on March 7, 1952, after concluding his speech at a banquet held in honor of H. E. Binay R. Sen, Ambassador of India.

The great world teacher demonstrated the value of yoga (scientific techniques for God-realization) not only in life but in death. Weeks after his departure his unchanged face shone with the divine luster of incorruptibility.

Mr. Harry T. Rowe, Los Angeles Mortuary Director, Forest Lawn Memorial-Park (in which the body of the great master is temporarily placed), sent Self-Realization Fellowship a notarized letter from which the following extracts are taken:

"The absence of any visual signs of decay in the dead body of Paramahansa Yogananda offers the most extraordinary case in our experience.... No physical disintegration was visible in his body even twenty days after death.... No indication of mold was visible on his skin, and no visible desiccation (drying up) took place in the bodily tissues. This state of perfect preservation of a body is, so far as we know from mortuary annals, an unparalleled one.... At the time of receiving Yogananda's body, the Mortuary personnel expected to observe, through the glass lid of the casket, the usual progressive signs of bodily decay. Our astonishment increased as day followed day without bringing any visible change in the body under observation. Yogananda's body was apparently in a phenomenal state of immutability....

"No odor of decay emanated from his body at any time.... The physical appearance of Yogananda on March 27th, just before the bronze cover of the casket was put into position, was the same as it had been on March 7th. He looked on March 27th as fresh and as unravaged by decay as he had looked on the night of his death. On March 27th there was no reason to say that his body had suffered any visible physical disintegration at all. For these reasons we state again that the case of Paramahansa Yogananda is unique in our experience."

Aims and Ideals

of Yogoda Satsanga Society of India
As set forth by
Sri Sri Paramahansa Yogananda, Gurudeva and Founder
Sri Sri Mrinalini Mata, Sanghamata and President

To disseminate among the nations a knowledge of definite scientific techniques for attaining direct personal experience of God.

To teach that the purpose of life is the evolution, through selfeffort, of man's limited mortal consciousness into God Consciousness; and to this end to establish Yogoda Satsanga temples for God-communion, and to encourage the establishment of individual temples of God in the homes and in the hearts of men.

To reveal the complete harmony and basic oneness of original Yoga as taught by Bhagavan Krishna and original Christianity as taught by Jesus Christ; and to show that these principles of truth are the common scientific foundation of all true religions.

To point out the one divine highway to which all paths of true religious beliefs eventually lead: the highway of daily, scientific, devotional meditation on God.

To liberate man from his threefold suffering: physical disease, mental inharmonies, and spiritual ignorance.

To encourage "plain living and high thinking"; and to spread a spirit of brotherhood among all peoples by teaching the eternal basis of their unity: kinship with God.

To demonstrate the superiority of mind over body, of soul over mind.

To overcome evil by good, sorrow by joy, cruelty by kindness, ignorance by wisdom.

To unite science and religion through realization of the unity of their underlying principles.

To advocate cultural and spiritual understanding between East and West, and the exchange of their finest distinctive features.

To serve mankind as one's larger Self.

BOOKS BY PARAMAHANSA YOGANANDA

* Autobiography of a Yogi
* Man's Eternal Quest
* The Divine Romance
* Journey to Self-realization
* Wine of the Mystic
* Whispers from Eternity

* Metaphysical Meditations
* Where There is Light
* Scientific Healing Affirmations
* The Law of Success
* How You Can Talk With God
* Inner Peace

* God Talks With Arjuna: The Bhagavad Gita
(A New Translation and Commentary)

AUDIO RECORDINGS OF PARAMAHANSA YOGANANDA

* Beholding the One in All
* Awake in the Cosmic Dream
* The Great Light of God
* To Make Heaven on Earth

* Be a Smile Millionaire
* Chants and Prayers
* Songs of My Heart
* In the Glory of Spirit

* Self-Realization: The Inner and the Outer Path

OTHER PUBLICATIONS FROM YOGODA SATSANGA SOCIETY OF INDIA

* The Holy Science *by Sri Sri Swami Sri Yukteswar Giri*
* Only Love: Living the Spiritual Life in a Changing World
  by Sri Sri Daya Mata
* Finding the Joy Within You: Personal Counsel for God-Centered
  Living *by Sri Sri Daya Mata*
* Enter the Quiet Heart: Creating a Loving Relationship
  With God *by Sri Sri Daya Mata*
* God Alone: The Life and Letters of a Saint *by Sri Gyanamata*
* "Mejda": The Family and the Early Life of Sri Sri Paramahansa
  Yogananda *by Sananda Lal Ghosh*

Some of the above-mentioned books are also published in Assamese, Bengali, Gujarati, Hindi, Kannada, Malayalam, Marathi, Nepali, Odia, Tamil, Telugu, Sanskrit, and Urdu. For a complete list of books and audio cassettes write to Yogoda Satsanga Society of India at the address given below. Also available are black-and-white and color pictures of Sri Sri Paramahansa Yogananda.

Available at your local bookstore or from:

Yogoda Satsanga Society of India

Paramahansa Yogananda Path, Ranchi 834 001, Jharkhand
Tel. (0651) 2460071, 2460074, 2461578
www.yssbooks.org

Yogoda Satsanga Lessons

The *Yogoda Satsanga Lessons* are unique among Paramahansaji's writings in that they give his step-by-step instructions in yoga techniques for God-realization. The simple yet highly effective methods taught in the Lessons enable one to harmonize and recharge the body with life energy; to awaken the unlimited power of the mind; and, above all, to achieve direct, personal experience of God through the *Kriya Yoga* science of meditation.

In addition, the Lessons cover a broad range of other subjects — offering inspiration and practical guidance for living every day in greater harmony with oneself and others, and for coping with the multitude of problems that seem so pressing in today's world. A few of the many topics covered are:

For free Introductory Literature, please write or call:
Yogoda Satsanga Society of India
Paramahansa Yogananda Path
Ranchi 834 001, Jharkhand
Tel: (0651) 2460071, 2460074, 2461578
www.ysslessons.org